PARKER, V.

Who are you? : in the polar lands

Please return or renew this item by the last date shown.
You may renew items (unless they have been requested
by another customer) by telephoning, writing to or calling
in at any library. ♻ 100% recycled paper   BKS 1 (5/95)

Who are you?
In the Polar lands

Vic Parker and Ross Collins

W
FRANKLIN WATTS
NEW YORK • LONDON • SYDNEY

Watch me waddle on
two flat feet.
I flap my flippers,
slip and slide, then…

Who are you?

Beware! I'm furry but fierce.
I run, climb and swim,
hunting with teeth and claws.
As I prowl, I...

Plodding on hairy hooves,
I scrape away snow to munch
on moss. My huge antlers are
handy for a…

I'm big and blubbery.
I fill up with fish,
then belly-flop on the ice to…

We all live in the polar lands.

Albatross

Musk ox

Penguin

Walrus

Reindeer

Polar bear

Arctic wolf

Sharing books with your child

Early Worms are a range of books for you to share with your child. Together you can look at the pictures and talk about the subject or story. Listening, looking and talking are the first vital stages in children's reading development, and lay the early foundation for good reading habits.

Talking about the pictures is the first step in involving children in the pages of a book, especially if the subject or story can be related to their own familiar world. When children can relate the matter in the book to their own experience, this can be used as a starting point for introducing new knowledge, whether it is counting, getting to know colours or finding out how other people live.

Gradually children will develop their listening and concentration skills as well as a sense of what a book is. Soon they will learn how a book works: that you turn the pages from right to left, and read the story from left to right on a double page. They start to realize that the black marks on the page have a meaning and that they relate to the pictures. Once children have grasped these basic essentials they will develop strategies for "decoding" the text such as matching words and pictures, and recognising the rhythm of the language in order to predict what comes next. Soon they will start to take on the role of an independent reader, handling and looking at books even if they can't yet read the words.

Most important of all, children should realize that books are a source of pleasure. This stems from your reading sessions which are times of mutual enjoyment and shared experience. It is then that children find the key to becoming real readers